TRUDEAU'S LIES MATTER

BR EDMUNDS

ISBN 978-1-7776112-2-4

Published by:

Kouski Publishing Canada

Ardmore, Ab

Canada

Prologue

I have been wanting to write this book for quite a while now but thought it would be ill received by most of the country who truly love kissing our Prime Minister's lying behind, but now that I really have pondered on it, I honestly don't give a crap. And our Prime Minister and his followers can promptly kiss my behind.

This book will be a listing of a number of Trudeau's lies as viewed and believed by me, and whoever wants to believe it. I will not state that they are defiantly 100% lies so not to tighten the rope that this government could surely put around my neck. But believe me that it can be verified and researched and you can make your own opinions about it. But we both know that they are lies.

Trudeau's Lies Matters will look at as many lies as I can fit in this book, of course I can't put every lie because I would need an encyclopedia series of books and frankly I have other things I would like to write about also. So for now, it's one book of Liberal lies, one book of Trudeau Faux Pas, one book of disgrace of the man in charge, one book of Communism at the Parliament, one book of a child in charge, one book of a man getting rich off of hard workers.

The worst thing about this man is that all the other countries worship him because of all the false information the media spews about him. He showed how easy it is to get the media on your side, you just have to take tax money and bribe the media with it. Which he did at a price of $600 million dollars. They post pictures about him getting his picture taken at his desk, and pictures of him FaceTiming his mother but never of him bribing, lying and cheating the system he is suppose to represent.

Don't get me started on illegal immigrants, that is a pile of crap on its own. If you criticize him about it then he will call you a racist. I am all for immigration, it is important for this country and that is why there are rules and steps to follow. These steps protects Canadians and makes sure that the immigrant can fend for himself and make a living without falling through the cracks. Now we are paying for hotel rooms and making hidden websites to try to find them jobs without the job seeking citizens to find out about it.

This man-child should go down in history

for the worst Prime Minister to ever lead Canada, but he will make sure to bribe enough media so this never happens. Let the lies begin, enjoy the book.

<u>***In the beginning, Electoral lies***</u>

Electoral Reform:

This was a lie that hurt a lot of people, and a lie that probably got him some votes from Western Canada in his first election win. *"We are committed to ensuring that 2015 will be the last federal election conducted under the first-past-the-post voting system... Within 18 months of forming government, we will introduce legislation to enact electoral reform."* This reform would have meant that the votes from Western Canada would have counted for something, Ontario and Quebec would not have decided every election and gotten all the benefits for doing so. We need a candidate that will promise and deliver this.

CTV had reported that *"Prime Minister Justin Trudeau is suggesting electoral reform might not happen at all, despite and election promise... He suggested there's less need for electoral reform now that the Conservatives are out of power."* Justin Trudeau is very good at blaming Conservatives for everything and this was not different. But how is it good if Conservatives are in charge but bad if Liberals are in charge? Trudeau is quoted with this crap;

"Under Harper, there were so many people who were unhappy with the government and his approach that people said, we need electoral reform in order to stop having governments we don't like". So basically Governments like the current Liberal Government that is only wanted by the Eastern Provinces as shown in the latest elections, if electoral reform was there, Trudeau's Communist Government would not have made it in at the 2020 elections.

Improving transparency:

Trudeau had promised to shine more light on Government by having full transparency and that anyone can see what his very public Party would be doing. According to a watchdog group representing Canada's Media concluded that it's worst then Stephen Harper's Government was to get legitimate information by this locked down Communist government.

This government finally got to changing the outdated access to information rules and according to people that tried to get information, it is harder to find, wait time is crazy and it will cost you more to get this transparent information from this "open to everyone" government.

Balanced budget:

Justin Trudeau had promised that the budget would be balanced and we would be sitting on a $1 billion surplus by 2020, what a crock of crap that was. He started throwing money around like he was a terrorist being paid off. He spent all the money he could to buy himself a seat on the U.N. Platform, even if that meant telling our soldiers that they were asking for more then we could afford. 2020-2021 numbers are at $1.2 trillion in dept, and before their cult followers jump on the Covid excuse, they were already at a trillion before the pandemic. When he was asked about how he will bring this down after 2 years of being elected, he answered his genius line: *"The budget will balance itself."* Wow, why didn't anyone else think about this instead of working so hard on a budget and spending $212,000 on a cover for the budget paperwork.

Trudeau is still spending like a starving child in a candy store, making sure that all the communist countries out there get a share and wishing he could rule a communist country also one day. In 2008 Trudeau had stated; *"With a dept-to-GDP ratio of 31%, we're not another Greece - nor do we need to fear turning into one. But with a structural deficit and no plan or timeline to get out of it, what we have is increased spending without any fiscal plan."* Funny that this is exactly where we are with this useless government right now.

Phase out subsidies for the fossil fuel industry:

This was an electoral promise that did not age well, not only is there still fossil fuel being extracted in Canada but Trudeau is buying a lot more oil from communist countries then he is buying from his own country. The man that was so against pipelines ended up buying a pipeline (which would have been built free of charge by a private company) at the cost of 5.5 billion dollars and then did nothing with it basically. What better way to stop something then to buy it and kill the project, he doesn't care it's not his money he is spending, it's yours.

He goes to the east of Canada to speak against fossil fuel and the pollution that it makes but then comes to western Canada and speaks about how good fossil fuel is for the economy of this country. After he goes to the far western province of BC and tells them that he will be sure to not let the pipeline go through their province and destroy the environment. I don't know how he keeps all this crap in line.

Promising clean water to indigenous people:

So this promise was suppose to reach results all over Canada by 2021. Well here we are and nothing has really been done. The numbers are crazy and Trudeau really was mostly accepted and received many votes from different reserves because of his fake concerns for this. Some advisories date as far back as 1995 that they have to boil their water before drinking it. As of now, 73% of First Nations' water system is either in high or medium risk of contamination.

In the year 2010, Justin's beloved United Nations declare water and sanitation human rights, acknowledging they are essential to the realization of all other rights. Many third world countries have jumped on this and assured clean drinking water for many places that have always struggled to have some but Trudeau's empty promise couldn't even bring it to some Canadian regions. March 2021 was suppose to be the deadline to fix all 105 long-term advisories, not counting the ones that were short term at the time but still have issues. Since the promise another 58 long term advisories have been noted. He lied about it in the first election and did nothing and on his second one he is slowly fixing but missed his deadline. I guess when you elect incompetence then you get what you pay for.

Revenue neutral carbon pricing:

This was an expensive joke on all Canadians, never seen such a web of lies just to add a tax. For those who don't know, a revenue neutral tax is suppose to lower other federal taxes to offset new federal revenues gained from carbon pricing. He thinks of getting away with it by not calling it a tax but a levy, In Canada you cannot tax a tax but you can tax a levy so you are paying GST on top of the tax, now this is crap.

He also gets away from this promise by forcing provinces to place mandatory carbon taxes and not hold them to revenue neutral tax so they can use the money for anything they like. After the economy crash his Carbon Tax is still rising yearly putting added strain and stress to all Canadians and the environment is not really getting any more help then usual. It's a tax scheme if I ever saw one, this guy is super delusional.

Reduction of greenhouse gasses:

Before his first win in 2015, Trudeau said that Harper's plan for cutting emission was not enough. After the election, Climate Barbie said that they will use Harper's ceiling numbers as their floor and work up from there. All these years later, Harper's floor is actually Trudeau's ceiling that he hasn't reached yet. They have had over 4 years to get things done but Cathrine McKenna seems to prefer taking selfies in nature and approving sewage dumps in lakes and rivers.

From 2006 to 2015 (the Harper years) the

greenhouse emissions by megaton was 730 (2006), 752 (2007), 736 (2008), 695 (2009), 703 (2010), 714 (2011), 717 (2012), 725 (2013), 723 (2014), 723 (2015). Given that they are not great numbers but they are still good numbers, more could have been done of course but it was never a big promise or a large part of the conservative's promises. Trudeau said he would crush these numbers and he didn't, even with his huge promise and putting so much focus on an Environmental Minister. His numbers from 2015 to now are nothing to what they want you to believe they are. His numbers start as 707 (2016), 716 (2017), 728 (2018), 730 (2019) and 726 (2020). So by these numbers, she basically sucks at her job. This is a promise that didn't age very well for the Trudeau government. The way that Trudeau talks about our emissions, it makes it look like we are the worst country in the world and if we reduce it then we can save the world. Canada is responsible for 1.6% of the world's green gas emissions but yet he wont buy clean Canadian oil, rather buy it from polluting countries.

<u>*I am a feminist*</u>

Trudeau has called himself a feminist many times, as he calls himself anything that will get him votes but this has been shown as a lie as he has at times treated women like total crap. Here are a few examples.

Elbowgate:

Justin Trudeau's manhandling of a female member of parliament had caused quite an uproar. The "annoyed" Justin Trudeau had stormed through a group of MPs to grab Conservative MP Gordon Brown by the arm and pull him out of the group. As he was pulling this man by the arm he was telling other MP's to *"get the fuck out of the way"*. Unfortunately New Democrat Ruth Ellen Brosseau had not gotten out of the way and Justin ended up elbowing her for her not listening to the "man" of the house.

Tom Mulcair, leader of the New Democrats Party, called the woman beater out by asking; *"What kind of man elbows a woman? It's pathetic! You're pathetic!"* And of course, he is right. Trudeau has always been pathetic. Of course he apologized three times afterwords because he couldn't let people think he wasn't a feminist even if he manhandles women when he gets frustrated.

Rona Ambrose, opposition leader, was quoted as saying; " *No one should ever have to deal with this kind of behaviour in any workplace. The fact that it's the prime minister of Canada is embarrassing. He should be ashamed of his actions.*" But is he, is he really? Brown, who was the MP grabbed by Trudeau, told the media; "*Let go of me, Now. Immediately afterwards, the prime minister went back down the aisle to confront other Members of Opposition. I later told the prime minister he should not have gotten out of his seat.*" After Trudeau's childish tantrum he finally found his seat without having to take his mother's hand.

I find that Niki Ashton hit the nail on the head with her statement; " *Not only was this the furthest thing from a feminist act... he made us feel unsafe and deeply troubled by the conduct of the prime minister of this country.*" This New Democrat's statement couldn't be more true that it is the worst thing a self proclaimed feminist could do.

Of course his liberal congressional followers, there all mighty and Devine leader could do no wrong. Liberal MP Judy Foote stated; *"I think you have to bear in mind that sometimes emotions run very high, but at this point in time I think we need to accept the prime minister's apology and recognize that civil obedience is something that we all appreciate."* A woman having to say this about this incident is sad but history tells us that Trudeau will get rid of anyone that speaks against him or his ideas.

Trudeau made his baby face apologies as usual but he had to make a few to keep face and not look like a total tool. *"I admit I came in physical contact with a number of members as I extended my arm, including someone behind me who I did not see. If anyone feels that they were impacted by my actions, I completely apologize. It was not my intention to hurt anyone."* Pretty sure that the woman you impacted with feels impacted by your action. Trudeau later apologized directly to the woman he abused, Brosseau. *"I want to take the opportunity to be able to express directly to her my apologies for my behaviour and my actions, unreservedly. I noticed that the whip opposite was being impeded in his progress, I took it upon myself to go and assist him forward, which I can now see was inadvisable as a course of action that resulted in physical contact in this House that we can all accept was unacceptable."* To me it sounded that he tried to make excuses in his apology, in my opinion I don't think he knows what he did wrong.

If you want to read more about elbowgate, and there is more to read, then check out **The Gardian**. They are a great news outlet that was not affected by the Trudeau Media Bribes and they really tell you how it is in the government no matter what side is in hot water. Check them out and show them some support.

Always believe a woman about abuse

So the man who is so behind women, so for the #metoo movement. Trudeau who was quoted as saying that all women who come forward with complaints of sexual assault and harassment should be believed. Trudeau's zero tolerance on misconduct was used on a few MP's.

When some conservative MLA's were rumoured to have said some harassing remarks they were told to step down. The sexual misconducts were taken very seriously and they stepped down before any investigation was even started. A Nova Scotia PC leader was forced out as party leader and later resigned on allegations of sexual harassment. Trudeau had mentioned that the idea of a code of conduct introduced to MP's before they take place in the House of Commons was interesting. (He would have broken most of the things on it anyway.)

When asked about the independent investigations toward MP's he said that if allegations surfaced against hi that the same standards would apply. But he went on by saying that he is very careful and no women would be able to accuse him of the kinds of behaviour of that kind. He has stated that; *"I've been very careful all my life to be thoughtful, to respect people's space and people's headspace. This is something that I'm not new to. I've been working on issues around sexual assault for over 25 years."*

This egotistical leader felt like he was slapped in the face when a reporter accused him of sexual assault. He had this "how dare you. Don't you know I'm a God" look on his face for the following days. Funny how this was in an editorial of a news paper 18 years prior to her answering questions, but I thought he had been careful for 25 years, probably careful to hide evidence. The reporter said that she had not taken action then and won't plan on taking any in the future. Of course Trudeau respects her decision but remembers the encounter differently, but what about believing the victims?

Of course after this, Trudeau said that he did a lot of reflection, or trying to find a good excuse. After pondering on the point he said; "*I am confident that I did not act inappropriately but I think the essence of this is that people can experience interactions differently.*" So do we still always believe the victim?

Strong women

So Trudeau, when he was elected, made a cabinet including 15 men and 15 women because it's 2015. That tells me that some people might have been chosen for gender instead of having the best person for the job. But the Elbowgate Prime Minister didn't appreciate strong women in charge so much after the Lavalin incident. One of these amazing woman was Jody Wilson-Raybould, who showed everyone that not all superheroes wear capes.

After showing and proving that the

Liberal Government was involved in the Lavalin scandal. Jody WIlson-Raybould, attorney general, and Jane Philpott who was the treasury board president, were both fired for telling the truth. So basically, Jody was being forced to step in and resolve the corruption and fraud case against SNC-Lavalin Group so the Montreal company doesn't face prosecution. Trudeau making Quebec's criminal seem legit.

The liar, I mean Trudeau, repeatedly denied any involvement from him or any of his senior lackeys. But that was proven otherwise that he might have violated Section 9 of the

Conflict or Interest Act. At this time even Trudeau's smoking buddy, Gerald Butts resigned from principal secretary to Trudeau also jumped ship. Followed by Michael Wernick, former clerk of the Privy Council. Innocent people don't quit such great jobs.

Wilson-Raybould appeared in front of a justice committee in February 2019, where she testified that for four months she *"experienced a consistent and sustained effort by many people of the government to seek to politically interfere in the exercise of prosecutorial discretion in my role as the attorney general of Canada in an inappropriate effort to secure a deferred prosecution agreement with Lavalin."* So she was basically asked to break the law to help out this Montreal company. One of the conversations was with Trudeau himself that had lied about the implication.

According to CBC news they reported that " *in a conversation with Trudeau on Sept. 17 2018, and with Wernick in attendance, Wilson-Raybould claimed the prime minister told her they need to find a solution for SNC-Lavalin. She said he told her many jobs would be lost without a DPA, and the company would move from Montreal, that an election was coming up in Quebec and that he was an MP for that province.*" Wilson-Raybould also claims that 11 people from the Trudeau cabinet pressured her into getting involved after she made her mind up not to. This cost her her position and she quit the Liberals and went as an independent.

Of course Trudeau denied everything and called the attorney general a liar and when the RCMP tried to investigate they were blocked from interviewing potential witnesses in the Lavalin case because they were shackled by cabinet confidence. If you want a good listen, Just search the recorded phone calls from Wilson-Raybould and hear for yourself that she was not lying.

If you want more information about this fake feminist then you can read the amazing story from MacLean's called *"Is Trudeau a fake feminist?"*. It is totally worth your time.

The $10 million dollar man

On June 23 2021, Trudeau issued a statement on the National Day of Remembrance for Victims of Terrorism. He was talking about remembering the 329 victims of Flight 182 in 1985, and also the attack on the National War Memorial and Parliament Hill in 2014.

"Terrorists seek to instill fear in Canadians, divide us, and make us question our democratic institutions through their cowardly acts of violence." Sort of like the

Trudeau government, but there is more: *"Canada condemns all forms of terrorism. We will continue to work closely with our allies and international partners to prevent radicalization to violence."* Sounds good on paper, too bad that Trudeau thinks that people don't remember that his government paid $10.5 million to a terrorist accused of killing an American soldier.

"Why do you think it's OK to give $10.5 million to a person that killed a soldier?" a woman had asked in a town hall meeting. Trudeau pointed to the Charter of Rights and |Freedom and said; *"we have to stand up for everyone's rights, whether you agree with them or not.”* So terrorist are protected under the Charter, according to Trudeau.

Omar Khadr was imprisoned and apparently tortured in a US prison, not a Canadian one, after his capture. Trudeau still defended his action because Omar had dual citizenship and one of them is Canadian and the other is extreme terrorist. *“That when a government violates a Canadian, and Canadian's fundamental rights, and allows them to be tortured, there are consequences and we all must pay.”* *“The question is what the Government of Canada did or didn't do* *and that as a deterrent, as taking responsibility, and that as actually avoiding what could have been a $40 million payout at the end of the day was why we made that decision."*

Now I am no lawyer but if I had a sure win at $40 million, because apparently this terrorist had a sure win, would you take $15 million? I know I wouldn't, and any other government would have not even considered paying a man who killed an allied country's soldier. But Trudeau is not an ordinary man and he does very stupid decisions.

So the first part of this chapter is nothing but lies because he clearly does not care about what terrorist do, if he did then he wouldn't have made one a multi-millionaire.

<u>"Aboriginals have a Prime Minister on their side"</u>

Here is a lot more lies from the Prime Minister, Mr. Castro, I mean Trudeau. Trudeau started in 2012 to make himself a God for indigenous people. He was fishing for votes and starting that, I am on everyone's side and I accept everything. As usual they were lies to get votes, like so many other things are. He promised reconciliation if he was elected and then flushed the ideas once he was elected, at least until the second elections. He put together a team to investigate the deaths of over 6000 indigenous children and the abuse of many others in residential schools. The report announced that it had found Canada to have committed cultural genocide against Indigenous people and made 94 calls to action.

Any student from some provinces could have saved him a lot of money because it's part of history books and mentioned on many documentaries. It wasn't a big secret that Aboriginal people were screwed by the government and the church in Canada. Trudeau had to pretend to do something because according to thenation.com website, that has a good article about this, Indigenous people voted in record numbers to help

Trudeau win a majority government. Trudeau even told them that; *"You have a prime minister who is listening to you and who is looking forward to working with you and you have an entire government that is interested in moving forward, hand-in-hand, in true partnership."*

According to thenation.com (I know but I like their site) the plan for reconciliation included nation-to-nation talks, as well as promises to implement UNDRIP federally and increase funding for reserves that a still didn't have clean drinking water (in 2021, many still don't have clean drinking water). His narcissistic ass even appeared on the Aboriginal People's Television Network in 2015 to promise that the people would have veto power over resource projects set to take place on their land. Well since then, of course, he backed off and told them that funding was put off for years. When the Canadian Human Rights Tribunal ordered his government to compensate indigenous children who had been harmed by a child welfare program, Trudeau just ignored it, because you know, he is above the law.

In his first years in power Trudeau spent

nearly 100 Million dollars fighting First Nations in court during first years in power. That is a lot of money to waist for someone who was on their side. *"Justin Trudeau is more slick when he's talking reconciliation, but we see on the ground, we see in the course, we see in their legal battles this total toxic legal war that goes on outside of the eyes of the public,"* said Angus, a NDP MP.

This is not surprising to me since the Trudeau Government spent $110,336.51 in court fighting a teen over a $6000 dental bill. This aboriginal teen needed braces to stop chronic aching pains in her lower gums, an orthodontist had told her it was the best way to go and had installed them. When her mother tried to get reimbursement through the First Nations and Inuit health benefit program, that is their for such things, she was denied by Health Canada. She appealed three times and was denied three times. Like anyone with benefits would do, she took it to court.

The Judge, of course appointed by the government, found in favour of the government and said that he found it reasonable that the benefits don't pay for this service. It's weird because she did not do it just for appearance or to make her feel better about herself, it was done to save her from severe chronic pain. The decision is again being appealed so this will cost even more for the government but I think if the judge would have went against Trudeau then he would have ended up like anyone else who dare make a statement against him.

What is even dumber is that the department determined that this young girls case fell short after it consulted with four orthodontists of their own choosing but these doctors never examined or even saw the teen. So how would these doctors know if it was necessary or not? If you agree with this benefits program or not is irrelevant, it's in place so it should be used. If the government gave you benefits then you would use them and fight if you get screwed over so it's the same for this program.

Honey, I bought a pipeline

Another great lie by our Crime Minister is that he supports the oil and gas industry of the West. Now right there is a big crock of Trudeau, if pants lit on fire when someone lied, his would be cremated by now. Trudeau being so environmentally friendly and him supporting the oil fields offends many people, mostly liberals. He lies so much just to be on everyone's side that the story changes depending what Province he is in.

Let's start with the pipeline money waste,

because all it was was a huge 5.5 Million dollar hole that Canada didn't need and would have been free if Trudeau was in favour of oil and gas. The pipeline that has been stalled since the Trudeau purchase has now ballooned to $12.6 Billion because of delays that are not being taken care of. It takes Trudeau to buy a pipeline and lose money from it, he probably couldn't run a lemonade stand.

Of course Trudeau's lies differ depending of what province he is in. When it came to Alberta oil sands his lies just got bigger. He came to Alberta telling us how great the oil sands is for the country and how he bought a pipeline to support the industry. But when he was in Peterborough, Ontario before his visit to Alberta he told the people there that Canada needs to phase out the Alberta oil sands. When he was asked about it when he was in Calgary Alberta, he said he misspoke. That is a big thing to Misspeak about. You have to be an idiot or clueless, you chose.

In the same nation wide lying tour, he blasted to how the previous Prime Minister wasn't able to get a pipeline build and that is a huge lie. In the time that Harper was in charge four major pipelines were built, Trudeau's wacky tobacco must be pretty good. During Harper's reign, the Enbridge Alberta Clipper, TransCanada Keystone, Kinder Morgan Loop and the Eldridge Line 9B Reversal were built but I guess he forgot about those.

Trudeau's environmental promises clashes directly with his promises for a thriving oil sands. If you come and visit or work for the oil sands in Alberta you will see that the environmental impact is very low and the rules and fines when it comes to anything environmental. The laws are stricken and are being followed at all the locations I've worked at or visited.

<u>"Quebec's are better than the rest of Canada"</u>

Trudeau claims to be there for all Canadians, he claims that he is proud of the whole country. This is nothing but another one of his many lies. He is there for Quebec and throws a little over the border to Ontario. He is nothing but a peasant who thinks he's a god.

"Quebecers are better then the rest of Canada because, you know, we're Quebecers or whatever." This was, of course, ignored by the media when Trudeau came to the elections but it is a quote from an interview he did in

1999. Of course after the fact, the media said that he was just quoting his father. The media will defend this so called leader in any way they can, $600 million dollars goes a long way into buying media.

In an interview with Tele-Quebec, Trudeau criticized the Harper government by saying that if Harper's government was to be what Canada stands for then he would support Quebec's independence. So basically he mentioned that English Canada preferred what conservatives stood for but he preferred Quebec.

When Trudeau was asked whether he thought Canada was better served when there are more Quebecers in charge than Albertans he replied: *"I'm a liberal, so of course I think so, yes. Certainly when we look at the great prime ministers of the 20th century, those that really stood the test of time, they were MP's from Quebec. This country, Canada, it belongs to us."* What an egotistical maniac this man is. This was from an interview he did in 2010.

Then there was the time when Trudeau started answering English questions in French, angering many anglophone reporters and anglophones in general. The worst one was when an English question came about to how English speakers could get help to gain access to mental health services. You have to be quite an arrogant ass to make a point of your cockiness on such an important question. *"Thank you for using our country's two official languages, but since we're in Quebec I'll answer in French,"*. He said. The English speaking Quebecers in the audience were upset about the lack of support they had just seen from their prime minister.

<u>*Environmental lies*</u>

Trudeau hosting about his government meeting or aiming at meeting targets for reducing greenhouse gas emissions. Canada has never met one of these targets. With all of Trudeau's talking and taxing people to the brink of poverty the emission at the end of 2019 was down only 1.2% from 2005 levels. The tax doesn't seem to be working, I thought if we paid enough the emissions would drop.

The Trudeau government has said that

they invested more then 12 billion in the Trans Mountain pipeline will fund the energy transition to renewables. He is trying to play both sides of the coin and please everyone with this statement but it is crap. I never understood how he wants to reduce the impact on environment by phasing out Alberta oil and gas but Canada imports oil from communist or non environmentally friendly countries coming on huge diesel guzzling ships. He is undercutting our economy by not using Canadian sourced products.

Trudeau has decided that he will force a carbon tax on Canada and also to force provinces to implement one of there own. Living in under a communist tyrant is not as fun as movies make it look.

When it came to the carbon tax, the Trudeau government had made an election promise before the 2019 elections that there will not be a carbon tax increase past 2022. Of course after the election he broke this promise of course. His lackey, McKenna, announced that, "our position has not changed". So they are back to the plan to increase from $30 per ton to $170 per ton by 2030, they only stopped long enough to lie to Canadians to get re-elected. I guess the quote by Climate Barbie is true after all, "If you repeat it, if you say it louder, if that is your talking points people will totally believe it".

When the conservatives warned people on social media that the Trudeau government was lying and the tax would go up to at least $102 per ton, they were "fact checked" and told that the Conservatives claims were false and misleading. I guess even Facebook was in on the lie, or is a Liberal run social media. The Trudeau government later said that they meant that they wouldn't change it yet, that they will wait after 2022 when they have spoken to the Provinces. Well they haven't waited and have not spoken to the provincial governments, as the Trudeau way, they just did what they wanted.

He tries to appease the people by sending some of them a carbon tax rebate check. Some people are all for it, but you have to remember that you have paid more in taxes then you are getting back so you are still in the red. Trudeau gives you money out of your wallet and you are happy about it, there is something very wrong here. Trudeau claims that 80% of households are better off with the carbon tax because of the rebate check they get. If you calculate all of the exterior factors like paying more for fuel and indirect rise of the cost of food and other essentials then the numbers are actually 70% are worst off with a carbon tax in place.

His lies on illegal border crossers began with a tweet from this twit. He acted like our borders were wide open, a back door to bypass the nice legal way to become Canadian. *"To those fleeing persecution, terror & war, Canadians will welcome you, regardless of your faith. Diversity is our strength."* I have no issues with immigration, I get why people want to come to Canada but there are ways to apply and checks to make sure everything is done correctly and safe for other Canadians. It really sounded like Trudeau knew nothing about the long and difficult process of immigration, or he just didn't care. All he wants is to look good to the world. It's like a drunk teen on Facebook just writing the first dumb thing that comes to mind. Our immigration offices were already overloaded and Trudeau decided just to throw a wrench in the system and sit back.

When Trudeau decided that Mexicans don't need visas to enter the country it brought up Mexican claims for refuge to more then 1000%. The saddest is that they sold everything to come here and most of them will have to be sent back, thinking that Trudeau's tweet meant that the door was wide open.

We had immigrants illegally crossing in Quebec by bus loads, saying that their lives were in danger or they were facing persecution. They were coming from the United States where many of them had a status of one kind or another, they just didn't like the President. Trudeau turned a blind eye to so much of it, playing dumb. It came to the point where RCMP officers were given bellboy positions and were carrying luggage for illegal border crossers.

Of course Trudeau never fixed his major screw-up, true to the Trudeau way he just keeps throwing money at it. Booking whole hotels, booking arenas and anything else that could hold the number of crossers.

Of course you can't ask questions about what the hell he is doing because with Trudeau, the word of the day is "racist". When an elderly woman asked Trudeau when the federal government would repay Quebec for the cost of the influx of illegal immigrants coming in from the U.S. borders. At this point the Quebec government had already demanded that Ottawa pay the full cost of all services for the "irregular border crossers". The bill was up to $146 million in 2018. Trudeau responded very rudely to this elderly woman causing her of being a racist, idiots use the word racist when they don't want to answer a simple question.

Turning a blind eye to a major problem is the same as lying about it, it won't just go away by pretending it's not happening or attacking anyone that questions you about it. Liberals have really screwed up in this subject. All the money it cost to deal with illegal immigration could have been spent to help speed up the process and hire more people to deal with more applicants so more people could come into this country. Only after many complaints to higher-ups and some media outlets started attacking him that he made his apology, saying he should have answered in English and did not mean no disrespect.

Oh, that helicopter:

On the Prime Minister's website there is a guideline that speaks about sponsored travel. "No minister of state or parliamentary secretary, no member of his or her staff shall accept travel on non-commercial chartered or private aircraft for any purpose unless required in his or her capacity as a public office holder or in exceptional circumstances or with the prior approval of the Commissioner."

Trudeau and his family accepted trips on

Aga Khan's private helicopter so he could take one of his many many vacations. This time he was going on this spiritual leader with ties to many governments' private island, and of course Trudeau didn't go to the ethics commissioner before his trip. He thinks that he is mightier then God so why would he need to follow such rules. Trudeau had tried to keep this trip a secret but the National Post had reported that he was on the private island so he very reluctantly release the least possible information about it.

Funny how he had started out as he was

not aware that he was breaking ethical rules when he has been in or surrounded by politics all of his life.

Drink box water bottle thingy:

Trudeau is a big supporter of getting rid of single use plastic although there are many pictures of him with straws and drinking from water bottles but if you ask him about it then of course he would lie through his teeth. When asked the simple question about what the Trudeau family does to reduce plastic use, he came up with a genius answer: "We have recently switched to drinking water bottles out of water of… when we have water out of plastic… sorry… away from plastic, towards paper…like drink box water bottles sort of thing." I don't think he liked the unscripted question that he hadn't prepared a lie for. This was a blatant lie, he was searching so hard to what answer would be best for the views he was trying to sell. If you can't answer a question honestly just tell the public that you need a moment to think up the perfect lie.

Look at me, I'm negotiating:

Not only did Trudeau making Canada look like a bunch of idiots when he visited India, not only did he dress in a way that would disrespect them and make us ashamed that he is our leader. He is such a disgrace to this beautiful country that I love to call home. On this trip to India, he was suppose to negotiate investments from them into Canada. When he came back from this ridiculous trip he gave a very uplifting speech, I mean he had to make it look like his taxpayer paid family vacation was for something. You have to make it look good when you take dozens of vacations on a poor taxpayers dime. Trudeau made a big speech about how India was investing $1 billion in Canada and our industries. This was later found out to be that $750 000 000 of that money was actually Canadian money going towards India. So Trudeau went there to negotiate a deal for Canada and we are the ones paying them, now that's quite a negotiator we have there. Page 84 He tried to deceive all Canadians, did he think that people wouldn't notice. The Liberal owned media of course played it off as if he misspoke, that is quite the misspeaking. If you don't know the difference between pay and receive then maybe you shouldn't be in charge of a country. Global News is quoted as writing; "Trudeau initially said the entire $1 billion was money coming to Canada but his officials later corrected that it was a two-way trade number, with one-quarter coming from India Page 85 into Canada and the rest going the other way. More then half the $750 million Canadian investment in India comes from Toronto's Brookfield Asset Management, which is spending $480 Million to buy a 1.25 million-share foot office complex in Mumbai. Another $200 million comes from Fairfax India Holdings Corp. of Canada, which acquired a 51 per cent stake in the Catholic Syrian Bank in Kerala, India" Funny how there was no real talk about this before the Trudeau Family Saga went off on their all expense paid trip. Must have Page forgotten about telling people about that part, was too busy buying costumes.

Asking for more then we can give:

Previous to the elections, Trudeau had made a promise to the veterans just to get the military vote. You guys see a pattern yet? He promised to reinstate lifelong pensions for injured veterans. He pledged $300 million annually military support programs if elected. In all of this the Liberal government left $372 million meant for veterans to go unspent in the first three years. This came a few months after a town hall meeting in Edmonton, Alberta where he told veterans that they were asking for more then they could afford to give. The grand total of money "set aside" for veterans that were not spent on veterans was $477 million by 2020. Buy they are asking for more then the government could afford. The Trudeau government said that the money will keep being brought forward to the following years until it can be used. But with all the Liberal lies, how long before they spend it on something else and just say "oops, I misspoke". The veterans go without but we keep asking the military to do the impossible when it comes to defending this country.

Epilogue

Now in 2021 and Trudeau is still the crime minister of Canada, elections are coming up where he hopes to have a majority government again so he can just make decisions again without thinking of what Canadians want. When he had the majority government in the first election, this country was looking more and more like a communist country then a democratic one. In the second election he saw how the west completely gave up on him, how only Quebec and Ontario gave him his election hence the reason they get so much. In his leadership he snuck another agreement in for equalization payments that nobody heard of before it was already done. So even in the economic crisis that Alberta is in, we still have to give money to Quebec. It's beginning to feel like they are the mulching family member that sleeps on our couch.

The worst part is that he makes sure that Quebec hates the west even if Alberta pays for most of their infrastructure. This government will destroy this country and everything it ever stood for, it started with changing the anthem, lying every time he speaks, turning provinces against each other with different lies he spreads to different places. It's time to get back together and vote in a competent government, no matter what colour banner they are waving.

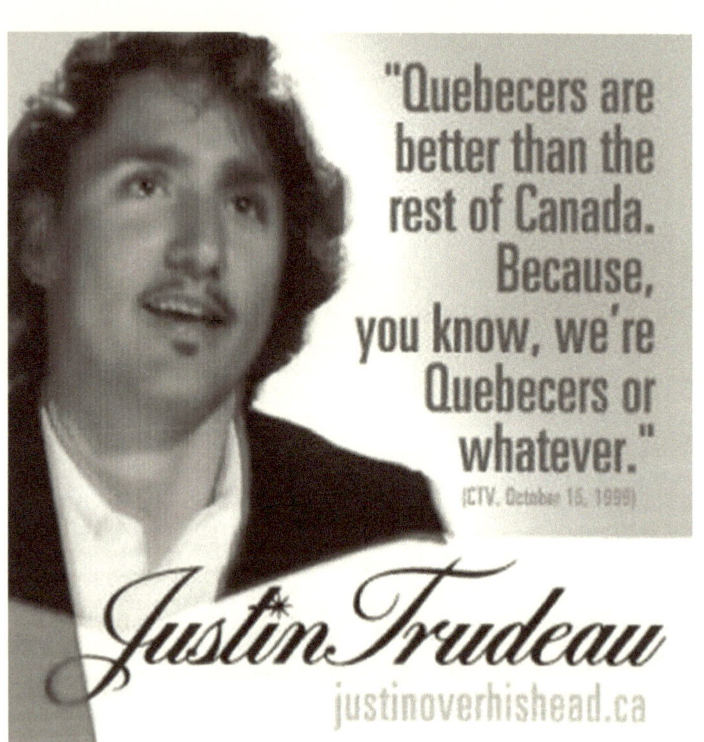

"Quebecers are better than the rest of Canada. Because, you know, we're Quebecers or whatever."
(CTV, October 15, 1999)
Justin Trudeau
justinoverhishead.ca

BR EDMUNDS

ISBN 978-1-7776112-2-4